I0824083

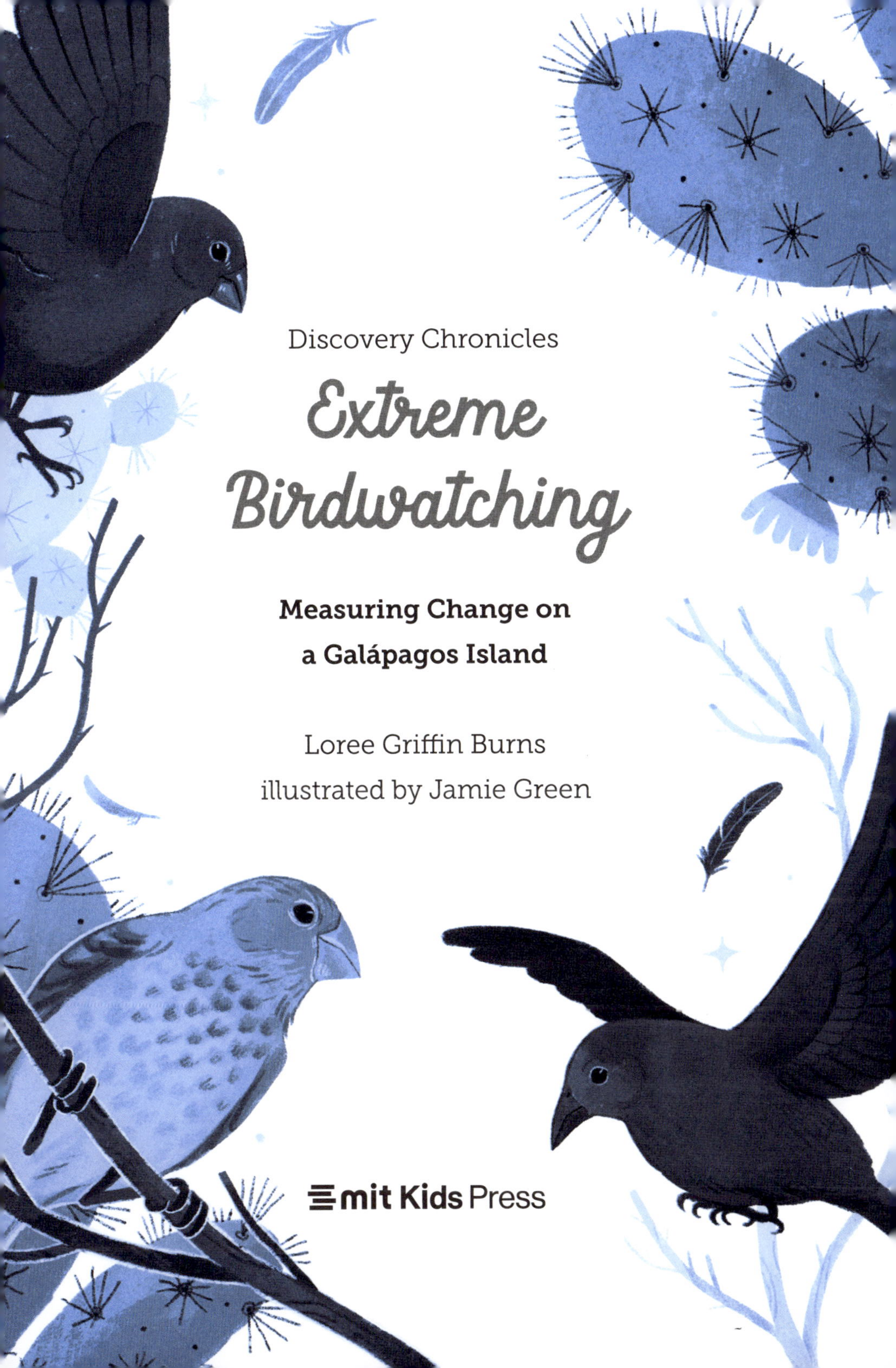

Discovery Chronicles

Extreme Birdwatching

Measuring Change on a Galápagos Island

Loree Griffin Burns

illustrated by Jamie Green

mit Kids Press

For Sarah and Kate and Linda, who reminded me that I can do hard things
LGB

For Angela—my friend and favorite biologist
JG

First edition 2026

Library of Congress Control Number: pending
ISBN 978-1-5362-3280-6

25 26 27 28 29 30 CCP 10 9 8 7 6 5 4 3 2 1

Printed in Shenzhen, Guangdong, China

This book was typeset in Museo Slab.

MIT Kids Press
an imprint of Candlewick Press
99 Dover Street
Somerville, Massachusetts 02144

mitkidspress.com
candlewick.com

EU Authorized Representative: HackettFlynn Ltd,
36 Cloch Choirneal, Balrothery, Co. Dublin, K32 C942, Ireland.
EU@walkerpublishinggroup.com

Contents

Introduction

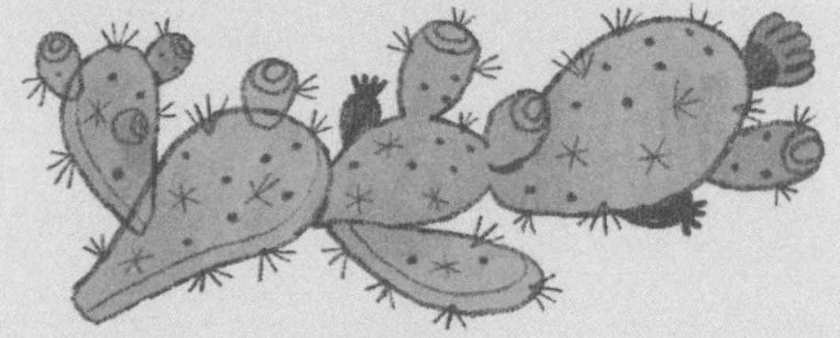

Daphne is an island. But not the sort you'd choose for a vacation. There are no sandy beaches, no trees tall or broad enough to make shade for humans, no resorts or hotels or houses of any kind. It's the top of an ancient volcano, circular in shape and less than a mile across. The base of the volcano lies deep under the Pacific Ocean. Its steep sides rise from there, ending, eventually, at a thin rim two stories above sea level.

Below that rim on the *interior* of the island is a sandy stretch of flat, dry ground that was once the volcano's crater. If you could somehow get yourself onto the island, up its sides, over its rim, and into that crater, you might be tempted to pitch a tent there. But the thousands of nesting blue-footed boobies who've already claimed that space would probably change your mind.

For all these reasons, most people who visit this part of the world sail right past Daphne. But there are an unusually determined and curious few who've stopped, who've gone ashore, and who've seen astonishing things there.

This is the story of those people.

Even more, it's the story of those astonishing things.

The water around Daphne is very deep and very clear. It's like looking into an over-crowded aquarium. It's full of fish. Turtles will come by. You'll see sharks basking and even an occasional whale passing.

B. ROSEMARY GRANT

I have had my toes nibbled by fish in the lagoon and pecked by a lava gull, and my right foot has been checked out by an octopus.

PETER R. GRANT

Quite simply, it was magical.

NICOLA GRANT

It feels like I was born there.

THALIA GRANT

One

THE JOURNEY

A human journey to Daphne starts with a flight to the country of Ecuador and, from there, a second, shorter flight to the island of Santa Cruz. From Santa Cruz, one must hire a boat. Scientists Rosemary and Peter Grant usually hire two.

The larger boat holds the Grants, their students, camping gear for everyone, food and water to last several weeks, and all the scientific equipment necessary to study Daphne's finches. (Finches are a type of bird. More on them soon.)

There is only one spot where Daphne's steep, volcanic sides flatten enough for someone to leap onto the island. Since the larger boat can't get close enough to this spot, a smaller dinghy, towed behind the larger boat, is handy. At low tide in a calm sea, the dinghy can get some of the people and some of the gear close to the three-by-six-foot (one-by-two-meter) landing place. There, dinghy bobbing with gentle ocean swells, someone—let's say Rosemary—perches on the boat's edge and waits for the right moment to jump. When she's gripped that tiny, barnacle-encrusted lava landing place with sandals and hands, she's ashore.

Once there, Rosemary turns to the boat to catch the gear handed or thrown to her by folks still in the dinghy. She stacks locked metal crates of food, plastic drums of water, sleeping bags, tarps, and more beside her on the

small landing. When the gear is unloaded, Rosemary scrambles up the steep slope so that Peter can leap ashore. Peter clambers up behind Rosemary and another brave scientist leaps out. And so on and so on until the dinghy is empty and there is a short line of people stretching up Daphne's volcanic slope, each about an arm's length from the other.

Someone pilots the dinghy back to the larger boat for another load of people and equipment. Peter and Rosemary and whoever has landed on Daphne with them start hauling gear—bucket-brigade style—up the slope to the slightly flatter plateau on the rim of the island.

Assembling all the scientists and all their gear on this plateau takes several trips and the better part of a day. Because Daphne sits on the equator, it's almost always a stiflingly hot day. Without a lick of shade to rest in, the team summons its strength and sets up camp instead.

Their journey—from waking up in their own beds and heading to the airport near home to crawling into a sleeping bag under a tarp erected on Daphne's rim—takes two days.

IT'S NOT AN IMPOSSIBLE TRIP.
JUST A COMPLICATED ONE.

GALÁPAGOS

Daphne is one of a collection of volcanic islands straddling the equator 600 miles (966 kilometers) off the west coast of South America. Known as the Galápagos Islands, they are part of the country of Ecuador.

Daphne's full name is Daphne Major, to distinguish it from the smaller and even harder-to-reach island, Daphne Minor, less than 4 miles (6.5 kilometers) away. Although people live on the islands of San Cristóbal, Santa Cruz, and Isabela today, none of the other Galápagos islands are home to humans.

Birds?

They live and breed on all of the Galápagos islands, including Daphne.

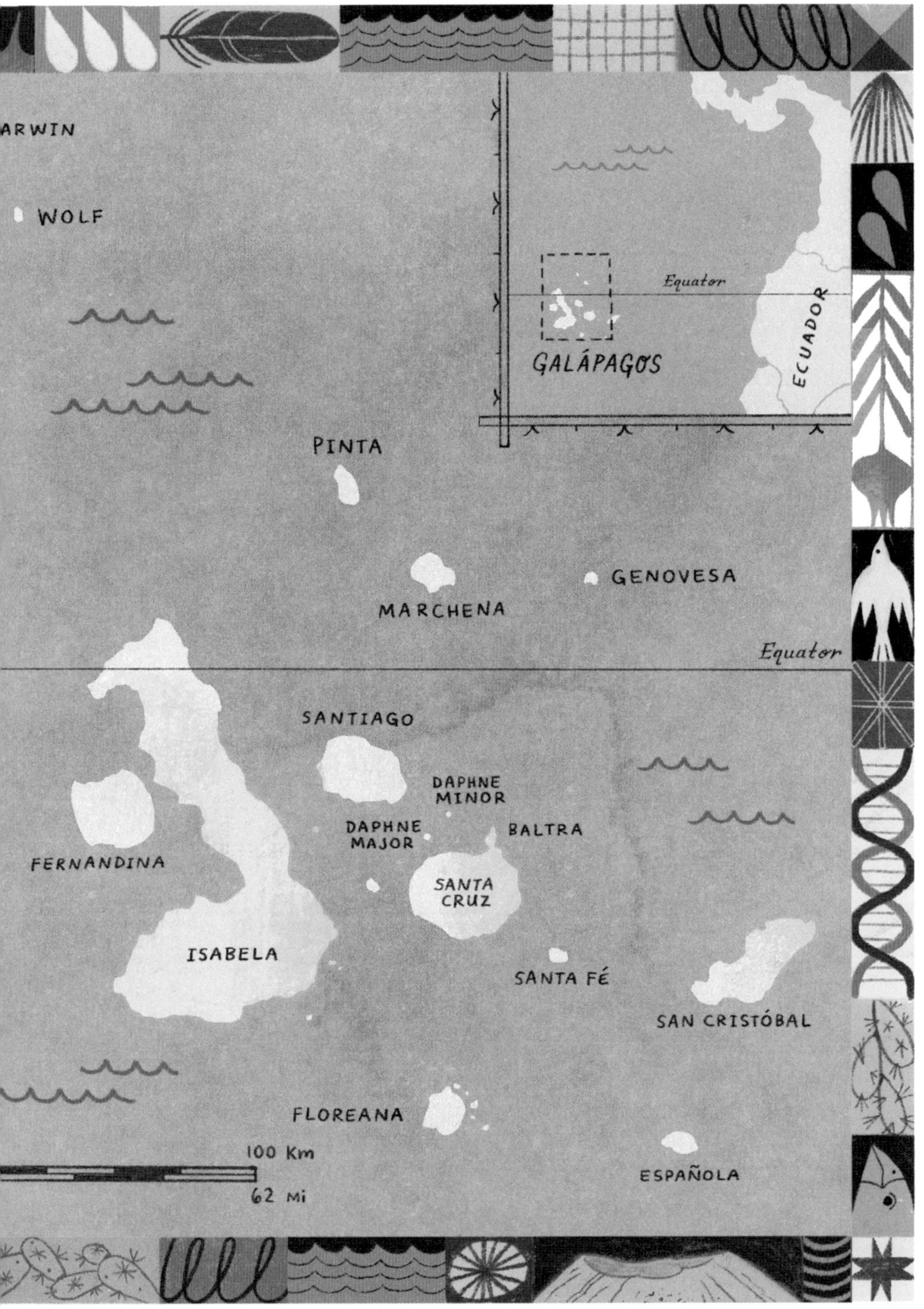
ARWIN
WOLF
Equator
ECUADOR
GALÁPAGOS
PINTA
GENOVESA
MARCHENA
Equator
SANTIAGO
DAPHNE MINOR
DAPHNE MAJOR
BALTRA
FERNANDINA
SANTA CRUZ
ISABELA
SANTA FÉ
SAN CRISTÓBAL
FLOREANA
100 Km
62 Mi
ESPAÑOLA

Two

DAPHNE'S FINCHES

The Galápagos are home to at least thirteen different species of finches, none of them found anywhere else in the world. Of these thirteen, only two—the medium ground finch and the common cactus finch—were living on Daphne when Rosemary and Peter Grant and their

team first arrived. Studying two species of birds at once is much simpler than studying thirteen species at once. This is one of the reasons the Grants chose Daphne for their work.

Scientists call the medium ground finch *Geospiza fortis*, or *fortis* for short. The common cactus finch is *Geospiza scandens*, or *scandens*. If you had a young fortis in one hand right now and a young scandens in the other, you'd have trouble telling them apart. Almost anyone would. Both are smallish, brownish birds with streaky breasts and orange beaks. As they age, the males of both species get darker in color, eventually reaching a fully black plumage. Both species build domed nests in

the same places, mostly cactus shrubs, and these nests are similar in size and shape.

If you were able to spend many weeks each year closely studying *fortis* and *scandens* on Daphne, however, you'd notice some differences. Their beaks, for example: *fortis* has a shorter, deeper one, while *scandens* has a longer, shallower, and pointier one.

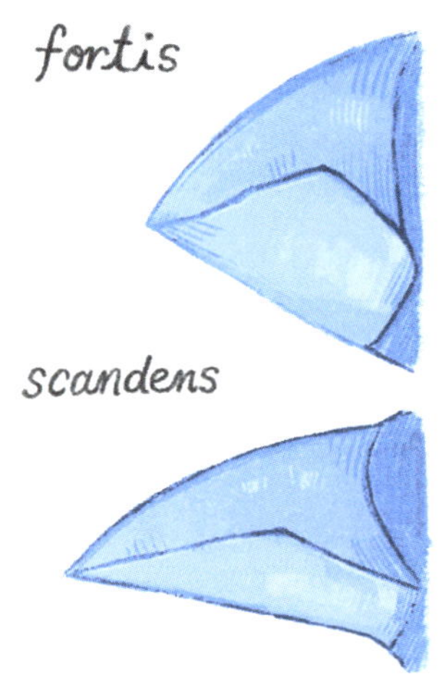

When the Grants first arrived on Daphne in 1973, they hoped the island would be a good place to learn how these beak differences affect the lives of finches. They planned to do that by getting to know every single finch that lives on Daphne. Every *fortis*. Every *scandens*.

How many finches is that, exactly?

The total varies from year to year, but we're talking several hundred.

How does one get to know hundreds of individual birds and their beaks?

Well, the first step is to set up a mist net.

After that, you take it bird by bird.

Three

FINCH BODIES

A mist net is a simple bird-catching tool: lightweight, plastic netting stretched between two tall poles.

The Grants and their team of finch-watchers stake the poles of their mist net into the ground near the cactus bushes where the finches roost and nest. They do this very early in the morning before the finches are active. As the finches wake and leave those bushes, they fly right into the hard-to-see netting. The holes in the netting are small enough that finch heads fit through, but not entire finch bodies. The plastic is soft enough that tangled birds aren't hurt while they wait to be removed.

The finch-watchers collect tangled birds as quickly as possible, to spare them the stress of being stuck when the hot sun rises. They slip each bird into a soft cloth bag. And when they've cleared the mist net, they bring the bagged finches to a shallow cave on the island's inner slope. The cave is shady in the early part of the day, which makes it a comfortable place to sit and study finches. The bagged birds are laid gently in the shade of this cave while the scientists have a quick cup of coffee and gather the tools they'll need next.

What do the finches think of all this? They're surprisingly calm. The scientists are gentle with the small birds, careful to keep wings tucked close to bodies and bodies oriented upside down whenever possible. This keeps the birds relaxed during their extraction from the mist net, their trip to the cave in a cloth sack, and everything that comes after that, too.

The scientists start by giving the birds names. Or, rather, numbers. A small metal band inscribed with a unique number is pinched onto one leg of each finch. A colored plastic band is added to that same leg. If that colored band is fixed below the numbered band—closer to the bird's foot—the scientists have determined the finch is a *fortis*. If that colored band is fixed above the metal band—closer to the bird's body—then the finch is a *scandens*. This system allows scientists to know which species they're looking at, even when the bird is far away. Perched on a cactus shrub, for example, or foraging for seeds on the ground.

There's more to this system. Colored bands are pinched onto the second leg of each finch, too. The bands come in ten colors. And each color represents a different number; black is the number 0, for example, blue is the number 1, and white is the number 8.

To know a finch's number up close, one can read the number on the metal band. And to know a finch's number from afar, an observer need only see the colored leg bands and "read" them in order from top to bottom on each leg, starting on the leg with the metal band.

Once a bird has been numbered, the scientists collect other information: the color of its feathers (this gives an estimate of age, especially for males), its sex, and

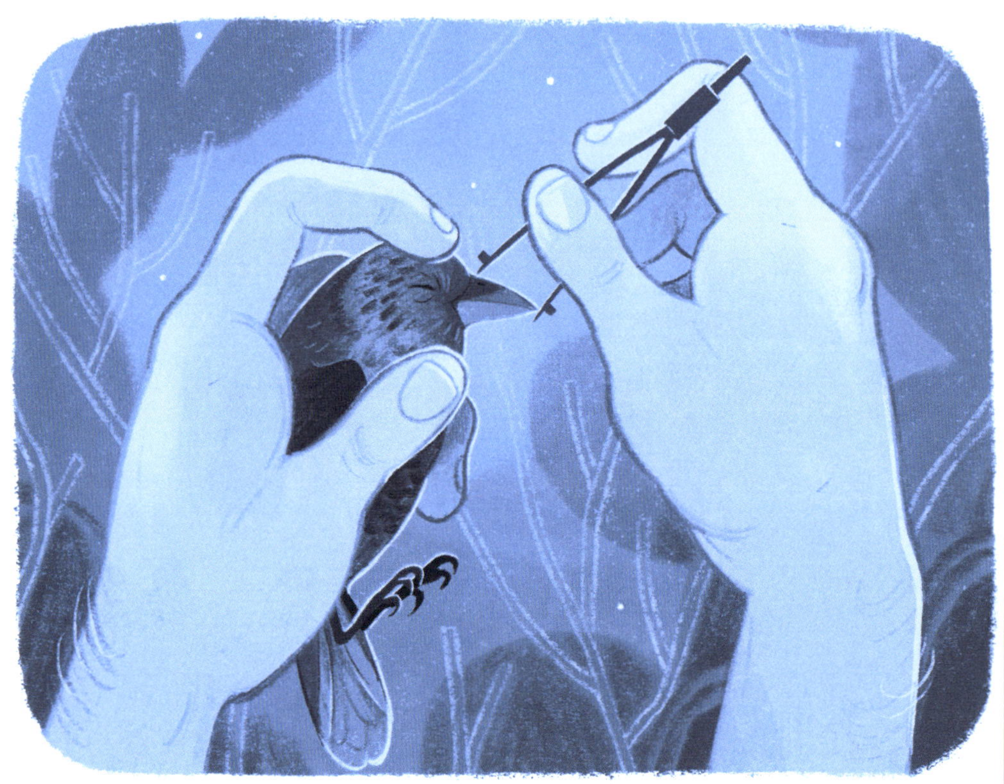

its relative health. Each bird is weighed on a scale, and the length of one wing is measured with a ruler. Special marked tweezers—called dividers—are used to measure the length of the beak, and another tool, called a caliper, is used to measure the depth and width of the beak, too.

Many years into the project, the finch-watchers added another item to the list of their getting-to-know-the-finches chores. In addition to banding, weighing, measuring, and recording the finches' body parts, scientists collected a single drop of blood from each bird.

When they began collecting blood, no one was quite sure what it might be used for. But it was easy to do and harmless to the finch. And so, a drop of blood was taken. The drop was preserved for something. For someday.

After all this identifying, banding, weighing, measuring, and preserving, the finches are released, free to go about their finch-y business.

And once they've cleared their tools and empty cloth bags out of the cave, the scientists are free to watch and record that finch-y business.

WET AND DRY

There are two parts to a year in the Galápagos: the wet season and the dry season.

The wet season begins sometime in December or January and lasts through May. The amount of rain that falls during that time varies, but because every living thing on the island requires water, the arrival of rain sparks a lot of change. Long-dormant plants and seeds begin to grow, eventually producing buds, flowers, and more seeds. Insects and other animals turn their attention to mating and reproducing.

When the rains stop, growth and reproduction stop, too. From June through November, days on Daphne grow progressively hotter and drier. Spent plants shrivel and die, leaving behind seeds that will, when the rains return, start the plant life cycle all over again. Likewise, animals turn their attention from producing young to surviving the drier weather and the dwindling food supply that comes with it.

Four

FINCH LIVES

What, exactly, do finches do all day?

The answer depends on what time of year it is. In the rainy season, the island comes alive with plants and insects, making it suddenly a rather excellent place to raise baby finches. So adult *fortis* and *scandens* get busy with the hard work of doing that. They find mates, build nests, lay eggs, and then feed and care for the baby finches that hatch from those eggs.

The Grants keep track of all of it.

How?

Extreme birdwatching.

Each day, after the finches caught in mist nets have been studied and released, members of the team circle Daphne on foot. With binoculars.

Walking the sloped sides of an ancient volcano means rocky terrain. Depending on the amount of rain that has fallen, that rocky terrain can be dry, dusty, and slippery or covered with heavy and wet vines and grasses.

In comparison to walking, the watching is rather easy. In the breeding season, finches can be seen singing for mates (males) or building a nest (females and males) or laying eggs (females) or feeding hatched baby finches (females and males). These activities are easily viewed through binoculars. And if those binoculars can be focused on banded finch legs, then the watcher will know which finch is doing it, too.

As they make their way around the island, watchers note which finches they see and what those finches are doing, and they also record each new nest on their map of the island. If they can, they use colored string to mark the bush in which that nest sits. The string will make it easier to find and monitor the nest in the days and weeks ahead.

The scientists spy on these nests daily to verify which two parents built each one. Eventually, they'll peek into the nests, too, carefully recording the presence or absence of eggs. If there are eggs, they'll record how many. When the eggs hatch, they'll observe the baby finches closely. When the babies are ready to leave the nest (called fledging), the scientists give them each a number, band them accordingly, and collect all the usual body and beak measurements.

When their weeks on Daphne end, the Grants and their students will have done something extraordinary: met almost every finch, *fortis* and *scandens*, on the island.

IT WASN'T AN IMPOSSIBLE TASK.
JUST AN AMBITIOUS ONE.

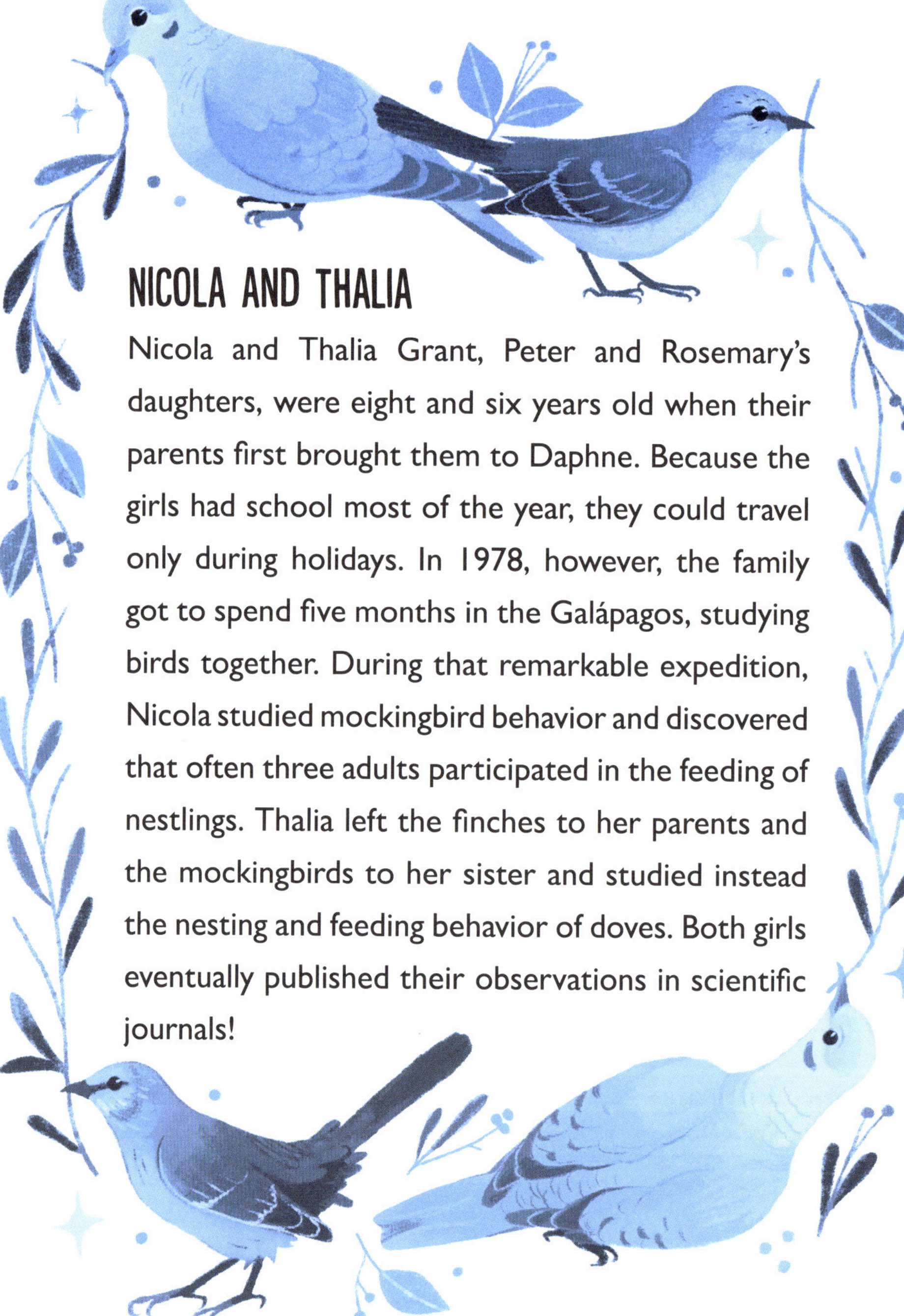

NICOLA AND THALIA

Nicola and Thalia Grant, Peter and Rosemary's daughters, were eight and six years old when their parents first brought them to Daphne. Because the girls had school most of the year, they could travel only during holidays. In 1978, however, the family got to spend five months in the Galápagos, studying birds together. During that remarkable expedition, Nicola studied mockingbird behavior and discovered that often three adults participated in the feeding of nestlings. Thalia left the finches to her parents and the mockingbirds to her sister and studied instead the nesting and feeding behavior of doves. Both girls eventually published their observations in scientific journals!

Five

FINCH FOOD

The Grants and their team visited Daphne year after year. In the wet season, they watched and recorded as finches mated, nested, and raised their young. And in the dry season, the team's attention turned to seeds . . . because that's where the finches turned *their* attention.

In the dry season, there are fewer insects, fewer buds and flowers and pollen and nectar and fruits. Seeds are the most abundant food left for finches to eat. And so, the daily walk around the island to observe and track nests becomes, in the dry season, a daily walk around the island to observe the seed-eating habits of finches. With binoculars, team members note every instance of a finch foraging or eating. Thanks to the colored leg

bands, they can record who is eating, where they are eating, and *sometimes* even what seeds they are eating.

Why only sometimes?

Because identifying a seed spotted only briefly in the beak of a finch is hard. Harder even than telling a *fortis* from a *scandens*. Unless, of course, you're willing to spend some time getting to know the seeds. And that's just what the team did next.

They started by roping off three large study areas, combing through each until they'd identified five individual plants of the most common species on Daphne. They tagged these plants with colored tape. They visited the study sites regularly, recording the height and growth pattern of each plant over time, as well as the number of buds, flowers, and seeds that formed. In other words, they studied the life histories of Daphne's common plants, just as intensely as they had been studying the life histories of Daphne's finches.

And they gave extra-special attention to the seeds. They recorded the size, shape, color, and texture of each seed type. They used a special seed cracker—a tool Peter Grant had designed expressly for this task—to figure out how much force was required to break open each kind of seed. And eventually, after many weeks across several seasons, the scientists were able to identify seeds on sight. They could identify them when they found them on the ground, and they could identify them when they spotted them in the beak of a feasting finch, too.

The extreme seed counting didn't stop there.

In each of their three large plant-study sites, the team mapped out smaller squares (about 10 inches by

10 inches, or 25 centimeters by 25 centimeters) for closer seed study. Using a hand trowel, they dug up the dirt in each square, down to a depth of about three-quarters of an inch. They spread this material in a shallow metal tray. And then they sifted through it grain by grain, pebble by pebble, and seed by seed, keeping close track of each kind of seed they found. In this way, they figured out exactly how many of each seed type were available in their small study plots at a given time.

And then they used these precise numbers to estimate how many seeds of each kind were available on the entire island.

THESE WERE NOT IMPOSSIBLE CALCULATIONS. JUST TEDIOUS.

WHAT DATA LOOKS LIKE

Much of the data that the Grants and their team collected was scribbled onto the pages of a waterproof notebook in the field as the finches were being banded or measured or observed. These quick field notes were carefully transferred from the small waterproof notebook into a larger and sturdier notebook, the Master Book, each day. Back home, the team transferred the information in the Master Book to spreadsheets on their computers: tables with rows and columns of numbers. Bird band numbers. Body weights. Wing and leg and beak lengths. Beak width and depth. And so on and so on and so on. From there, they developed computer programs to help sift through the numbers and look for patterns. What kinds of patterns? They weren't sure at first. But as they returned to Daphne year after year, diligently collecting the numbers, some rather interesting ones became clear.

Six

PATTERNS

After a few seasons of measuring finches and counting seeds on Daphne, the Grants and their team had collected a massive amount of information. They knew the body and beak dimensions of almost every *fortis* and *scandens* on the island. They knew the family histories of these birds, too. They knew how many seeds and which kinds of seeds were available to the finches at different times of year, and they knew which seeds were favored by which birds.

What in the world would they do with all this information?

Well, first they took it all back to their university offices.

Then they studied it carefully, looking for patterns.

What kinds of patterns did they find?

Here's one example: they noticed big *fortis* finches tended to have big *fortis* babies, and smaller *fortis* finches tended to have smaller *fortis* babies.

They noticed this related pattern, too: big-beaked *fortis* parents tended to produce young *fortis* with big beaks.

This result was not unexpected. We've known for a long time that animal parents pass physical characteristics on to their children. Golden retriever parents pass their yellow, silky coats on to their puppies, while Dalmatian parents pass on their black spots. Human parents can pass characteristics like their height, their eye color, or their pointed chins (and more!) on to their children. Finding this pattern of inheritance in the Daphne data verified that in finches, body size and beak size are handed down from one generation of birds to the next. These are inherited traits.

There were other interesting patterns in the Daphne data, too.

In the wet season, for example, when all seeds are plentiful, the data showed that *fortis* spend most of their time eating soft, easy-to-crack seeds. The data showed that *scandens* eat a lot of these seeds, too.

In the dry season, however, this feeding pattern changes. At this time of year, *fortis* were spotted eating the hard-to-crack seeds they'd ignored during the wet season. And what about *scandens*? They were never observed eating these hard-to-crack seeds.

The finch-watchers found this pattern particularly interesting. They knew that one of the main differences between *fortis* and *scandens* is the size and shape of their beaks. And because beaks are a bird's main tool for eating seeds, they wondered: Are the shorter, deeper beaks of *fortis* better at cracking larger, harder seeds? Is it possible that the longer, narrower beaks of *scandens* aren't strong enough to crack them at all?

Seven
DROUGHT

The Grants and their students had been collecting data on Daphne, its finches, and its seeds a few times a year for four years when something unexpected happened: the wet season wasn't wet.

In 1976, a typical year, the island was showered with about 5 inches (13 centimeters) of rain. When the team arrived in December of that year, as the dry season was nearing its end, they got busy watching finches and counting seeds the way they always had, waiting for the rains to start. But those rains never came. December was completely dry. January was completely dry. And shockingly, February was completely dry, too.

Without rain, the plants didn't produce the new growth, buds, flowers, or seeds they usually did at this time of year. Many of the plants died.

Without plants to support their life cycles, many of Daphne's insects didn't reproduce, either.

And without rain, plants, or insects, most of the finches didn't mate.

There was no rain in March, April, or May of 1977, or any month thereafter. By year's end, there had been less than one inch of rain on Daphne. The finch-watchers observed little nest building and little mating, few eggs and hardly any baby finches. What they saw instead was distressing: lots of dying birds.

They didn't interfere with this natural process, as much as they may have wanted to. Instead, they watched. They recorded. They counted. During all visits in 1977, the team saw finches struggle to find enough to eat. They found starved birds in large numbers all over the island. Because most of the birds on the island were banded, they could keep track of who lived and who didn't. They recorded these deaths as carefully as they had recorded the lives of the very same birds.

In January of the next year, 1978, it finally rained again on Daphne. The finch-watchers arrived soon after. They could tell the *fortis* and *scandens* populations were small, and they set about catching the survivors in mist nets. They weighed and measured survivor bodies. They measured their beaks. And they watched the finches respond to the rain by nesting, choosing mates, laying eggs, and raising young. Things had returned to normal, it seemed.

Armed with information collected during the difficult drought of 1977, as well as that collected during the months when the rains finally returned in 1978, the scientists headed home to analyze their finch and seed data. Interesting new patterns emerged.

First of all, a whole lot of birds had died in the drought. In 1976, there were about 400 *scandens* recorded on Daphne. By the end of 1977, after a year with barely any rain, there were only 115 *scandens* left. The numbers for *fortis* were similarly grim: the population of more than 1,400 birds recorded in 1976 was down to 181 after the drought.

Looking at seed data, all this death made sense. There simply weren't many seeds available on the island during the drought. For month after dry month, the island's birds ate up seeds left over from previous seasons. And since there were no plants producing new seeds, this supply ran low. Eventually the only seeds left were the biggest and hardest-to-crack variety.

How did *fortis*—the finches known to eat these seeds—respond? When the scientists looked closely at their beak measurements for *fortis* alive before the drought and compared them to the beak measurements of the *fortis* still alive after the drought, an interesting difference stood out.

The average beak depth—the measurement from top to bottom of the beak—of the population of *fortis* before the drought was 0.37 inches (9.42 millimeters).

The average beak depth of the population of *fortis* alive after the drought was 0.39 inches (9.96 millimeters).

In other words, the data collected before, during, and after the drought indicated that *fortis* with deeper beaks were the ones most likely to have survived the drought. This small but significant change in beak depth was the difference between life and death.

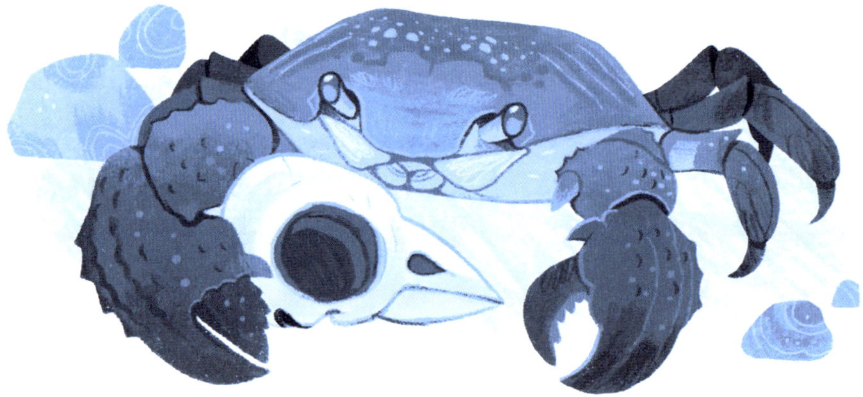

Eight
NATURAL SELECTION

Farmers who raise livestock have known for centuries that they can change the look of their animals from one generation to the next by carefully choosing which animals to mate. Interested in sheep with thicker wool coats? Select only those sheep with the very thickest wool for mating. And when the next generation of sheep is born, choose only those with the very thickest wool for mating again. This selective breeding, carried out year after year and decade after decade and even century after century on a sheep farm, will eventually produce a population of sheep with wool coats so thick that farmers from the century before might not even recognize them.

Likewise, one can create plants that produce tastier new vegetables or unusually colored flowers or wildly odd-looking leaves. For example, what we call broccoli today was once a leggy cabbage weed whose flowers didn't look anything like a head of broccoli. But when a plant with unusually large flower heads showed up in their gardens, growers used only that plant for mating (for plants we'd say *crossing*) and growing the next year. Over time, by carefully choosing only plants with the largest flower heads, breeders created the variety of cabbage that we now know as broccoli. The part we eat is the modified flower head.

This deliberate breeding with a focus on producing plants or animals with specific desired characteristics is called artificial selection. And the Daphne study proved that a version of this same process happens to organisms in the wild.

Instead of farmers or breeders choosing which animals to mate, a natural event did the choosing. We call this natural selection.

In 1977, the drought on Daphne created conditions in which plants didn't produce seeds. The island's finches ate through the small, easy-to-crack seeds left over from the previous season first, as those are their favorites. Eventually, however, those small seeds ran out. And what was left on Daphne were the bigger, harder-to-crack seeds. The *fortis* that could crack open and eat those seeds were more likely to survive. And these, it turns out, were the *fortis* with deeper beaks.

But there's more to the story.

When the rains returned and the next breeding season got underway, those *fortis* survivors—bigger beaked than all the other finches that had lived on Daphne that year—mated with the only *fortis* available. Which were, of course, also bigger beaked. And the young finches they produced . . . had much bigger beaks, on average, than the young *fortis* finches of any previous generation.

In other words, the process of natural selection had changed the species of finches known as *Geospiza fortis.* In a single, remarkable season they had become birds with slightly deeper beaks.

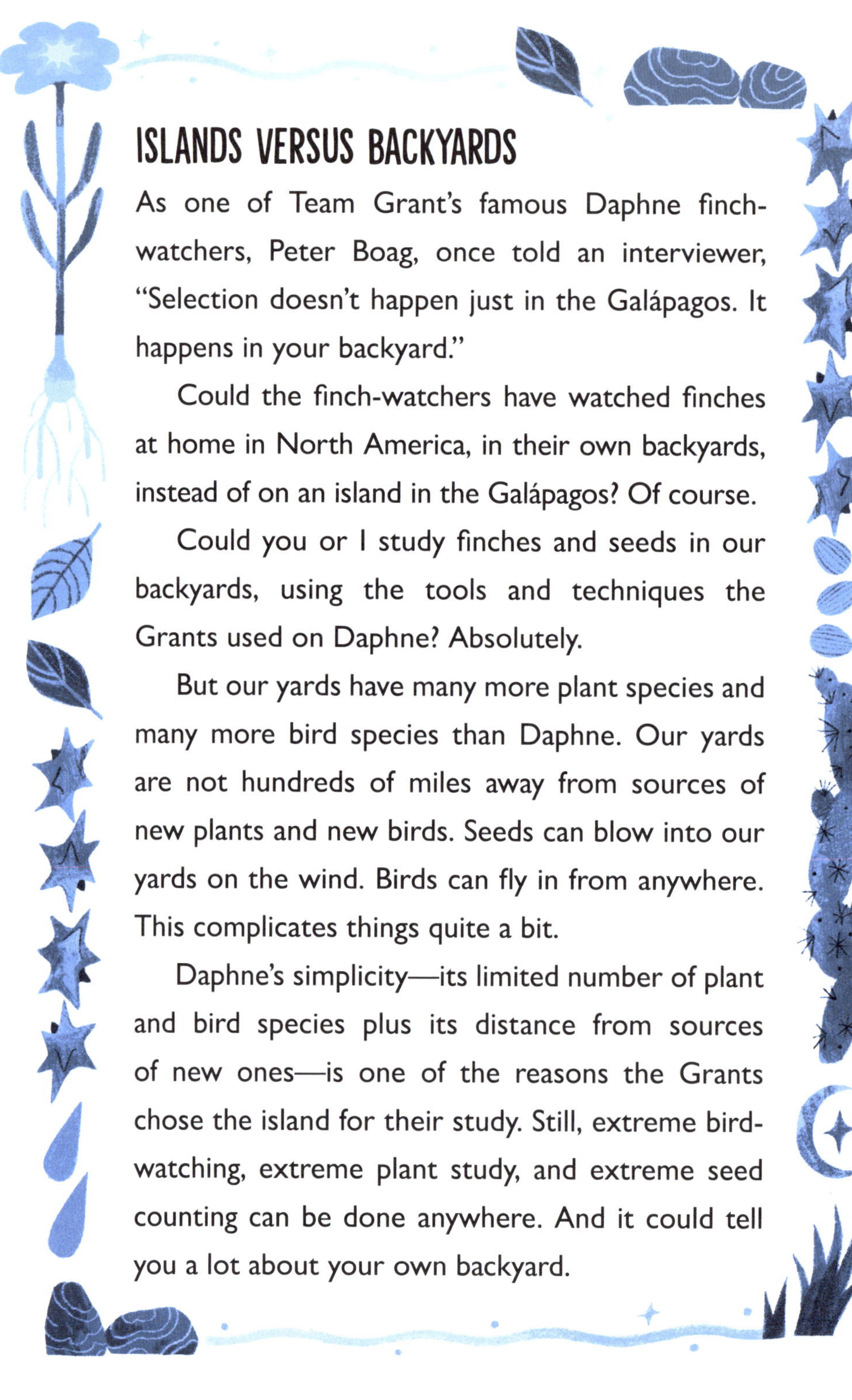

ISLANDS VERSUS BACKYARDS

As one of Team Grant's famous Daphne finch-watchers, Peter Boag, once told an interviewer, "Selection doesn't happen just in the Galápagos. It happens in your backyard."

Could the finch-watchers have watched finches at home in North America, in their own backyards, instead of on an island in the Galápagos? Of course.

Could you or I study finches and seeds in our backyards, using the tools and techniques the Grants used on Daphne? Absolutely.

But our yards have many more plant species and many more bird species than Daphne. Our yards are not hundreds of miles away from sources of new plants and new birds. Seeds can blow into our yards on the wind. Birds can fly in from anywhere. This complicates things quite a bit.

Daphne's simplicity—its limited number of plant and bird species plus its distance from sources of new ones—is one of the reasons the Grants chose the island for their study. Still, extreme bird-watching, extreme plant study, and extreme seed counting can be done anywhere. And it could tell you a lot about your own backyard.

Nine
SOMEDAY

Natural selection has been seen and recorded in the wild in other species, too.

Scientists have recorded changes in the color of the British peppered moth in response to the levels of soot in the air where those moths live. In sootier environments, darker-colored moths were more common. In environments with cleaner air, lighter-colored moths dominated. It turns out that moth survival depends on the ability of individuals to blend into the trees in their environment—if they don't blend, they are more visible to the birds around them and, so, more likely to be eaten.

Other scientists have documented changes in the size, number, and color of spots on populations of guppies, a type of fish, in response to the presence or absence of guppy-eating predators. When predators are introduced to previously predator-free, guppy-filled bodies of water, subsequent generations of guppies sport fewer, smaller, and less-colorful spots, making them harder for the predator fish to notice . . . and eat.

This list goes on.

And while scientists around the world continue to observe and study these instances of natural selection in real time, others are working to understand what underlies the process. What, *exactly,* is changed in the

bodies of peppered moths that makes them darker in color? What, *exactly*, is changed in the bodies of guppies that causes their spots to get smaller, fewer, and less colorful over many generations of living in predator-filled waters?

Now is a good time to remind you of the blood samples the Grants began collecting back in the early years of the Daphne study. Because those drops of blood are now being used to study the *something* that is changed inside finch bodies (and guppy bodies and peppered moth bodies and more) as they change across generations. And that something, it turns out, is deoxyribonucleic acid, or DNA.

DNA is an incredibly important molecule, some version of which is found inside the cells of every living creature on planet Earth. It is the basis of all inheritance, the thing that is passed from parent to offspring and that dictates physical characteristics—yellow, silky coats in golden retrievers, eye color in humans, beak size in finches, and more.

We now know that as DNA is passed from parent to offspring, changes are introduced into the molecule. If a change is useful—that is, if it helps an organism survive in its environment—then that organism is more likely to grow up and to mate. And when it does, its changed DNA will be passed on to the next generation.

The Daphne study was a finch-watching experiment. But now we know that its results reach beyond the island's shores and beyond its finches, too.

Natural selection leads to changes in physical characteristics that can, over years and decades and centuries and eons, give rise to entirely new organisms. This process, called evolution, is at work on all organisms on earth. Constantly. And it has been since the beginning.

THE LAST JOURNEY

After forty years of extreme finch-watching in the Galápagos, Peter and Rosemary Grant visited Daphne for the last time in 2012. By then, they and their many students and collaborators had banded 5,984 finches on the island.

Their Master Books of data still line the shelves of their offices in Princeton, New Jersey.

Their massive spreadsheets of numbers are still studied by students of natural selection.

And the blood samples they began collecting in the late 1980s are right now being used in laboratories around the world to better understand the evolution of finch beaks and the process of evolution by natural selection.

The two have won many awards for their scientific achievements and will likely collect more in the future. But for both Peter and Rosemary, the value of their life's work lies in the place they got to know so well, the extreme ways they got to know it, and the way this knowledge has helped us better understand how life on earth works.

Conclusion

Thanks to the finch-watchers and their four decades of closely monitoring Daphne's finches and their environment, we've learned a lot.

We've learned that beak size is a heritable characteristic in birds, for example.

We've learned that changing conditions can give certain birds an advantage, and because the birds with the advantage are more likely to survive, the characteristics that helped them to do so will be passed on to the next generation. On Daphne during the drought, this process led to *fortis* with bigger beaks.

We've learned that natural selection, over time, results in birds that are sometimes very different from the birds in generations before them. Given enough time and enough change, birds can become more and more different.

That's how the Galápagos got their many different species of finches in the first place.

We've learned that these processes—natural selection and evolution—can be observed in the wild. Especially if one can find a simplified system—an island in a remote location with a very limited palette of plants and animals—in which to observe them.

But we've learned other important and less technical things, too.

The astonishing power of human curiosity, for example.

The value of hard journeys and ambitious observations and tedious tasks.

The idea that sometimes the things that seem impossible are just . . . hard.

AND PROOF THAT WE HUMANS CAN DO HARD THINGS.

Author's Note

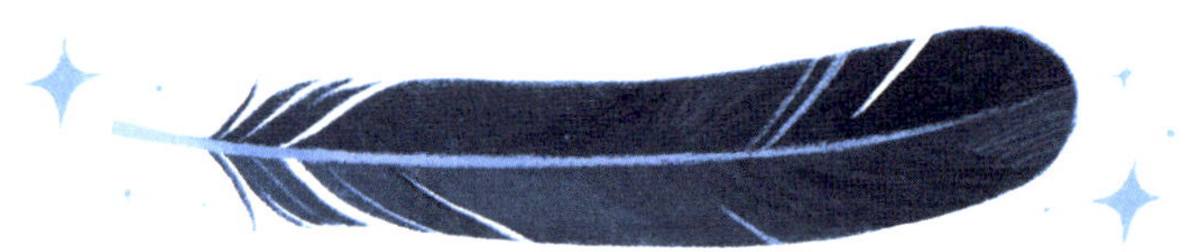

In this book, I've told a much-simplified version of Peter and Rosemary Grant's four-decade Daphne study story. I've had to leave out dozens of fascinating observations and discoveries, particularly those that had to do with *scandens.*

For example, only two species of Galápagos finch were breeding on Daphne in 1972, when the Grants first arrived. But by 2012, when they officially ended the Daphne study, there were more, including an interesting new hybrid species that the Grants call Big Bird. Also, it is now commonly accepted that there are seventeen species of Galápagos finch on the islands.

As another example, the Grants observed natural selection in finches several distinct times during their study. Not long after the drought of 1977, there was another natural event that led to a change in the size and shape of finch beaks: 1983 was the rainiest year in Daphne's recorded history; 54 inches (137 centimeters) of rain fell! The team collected data throughout the deluge, and at the end of it, that data showed evolution by natural selection again . . . but this time in the opposite direction of that forced by the drought. Birds with smaller beaks survived the floods better.

I hope you'll explore the work of the finch-watchers more on your own. Or maybe even do some finch observation work in your own neighborhood. I've included a few resources to get you started.

Glossary

ARTIFICIAL SELECTION: the process of mating only those organisms that display certain desirable characteristics in order to produce a new generation of animals in which this characteristic is highlighted

CALIPER: a tool with a sliding, adjustable jaw that is convenient for measuring the thickness of small objects, such as a bird's beak or a seed

CROSS: the joining of pollen from one plant with the ovule of another in order to produce a new generation of seeds

DATA: a body of information or collected facts

DIVIDERS: a type of caliper that has two movable arms that can be stretched apart in order to accurately record the length or the width of an object, such as a bird's beak

DNA (DEOXYRIBONUCLEIC ACID): one of the most important biological molecules found in living organisms; it provides the instructions from which other important biological molecules can be built

EVOLUTION: the change in a physical feature or trait in a population of organisms over time

FINCH: a perching bird with a small head and body, pointed wings, a forked tail, and a triangular beak

FLEDGING: in young birds, gaining the ability to fly from the nest and live independently from their parents

FORAGING: wandering in search of food. In this book, finches forage by exploring the island and scratching the ground with their feet and beaks.

INHERITED TRAITS: physical characteristics passed on from parents to offspring

MATING: the physical joining of male and female DNA in order to produce the next generation of a species

NATURAL SELECTION: the survival of the individual organisms that are best adjusted to their specific environment such that the traits that aided that adjustment are passed on to the next generation of that organism

NESTLING: a young bird that is unable to leave the nest because it has not yet acquired the necessary flight feathers; nestlings rely on their parents and other helpers for nourishment

PLUMAGE: a bird's full body of feathers, including their arrangement, colors, and patterns

SCALE: a tool for weighing objects. On Daphne, the Grants use a spring scale, with a spring fixed on one end and a hook on the other; objects attached to the hook pull the spring a distance that is translated into a measurement of weight on the body of the scale.

More to Explore

BOOKS TO INSPIRE EXTREME BIRDWATCHING

Choiniere, Joseph, and Claire Mowbray Golding. *What's That Bird? Getting to Know the Birds Around You, Coast to Coast*. North Adams, MA: Storey Publishing, 2005.

Roy, Katherine. *Making More: How Life Begins*. New York: Norton, 2022.

Wilson, Mark. *Owling: Enter the World of the Mysterious Birds of the Night*. North Adams, MA: Storey Publishing, 2019.

BOOKS TO GET YOU LOOKING CLOSELY

Burns, Loree Griffin, and Ellen Harasimowicz. *Citizen Scientists: Be a Part of Scientific Discovery from Your Own Backyard*. New York: Henry Holt, 2012.

Burris, Judy, and Wayne Richards. *The Secret Lives of Backyard Bugs: Discover Amazing Butterflies, Moths, Spiders, Dragonflies, and Other Insects!* North Adams, MA: Storey Publishing, 2011.

Helzer, Chris. *Hidden Prairie: Photographing Life in One Square Meter.* Iowa City: University of Iowa Press, 2020.

Silver, Donald. *One Small Square: Backyard*. Illustrated by Patricia Wynne and Dianne Ettl. New York: McGraw Hill, 1997.

BOOKS ABOUT EVOLUTION

Collard III, Sneed B. *One Iguana, Two Iguanas: A Story of Accident, Natural Selection, and Evolution*. Thomaston, ME: Tilbury House, 2018.

Davies, Nicola. *Many: The Diversity of Life on Earth*. Illustrated by Emily Sutton. Somerville, MA: Candlewick Press, 2017.

Patent, Dorothy Hinhaw. *The Lizard Scientists: Studying Evolution in Action*. Photographs by Nate Dappen and Neil Losin. New York: Clarion, 2022.

Pringle, Laurence. *Billions of Years, Amazing Changes: The Story of Evolution*. Honesdale, PA: Boyds Mills Press, 2011.

Thomas, Isabel, and Daniel Egnéus. *Moth: An Evolution Story*. London: Bloomsbury, 2019.

BOOKS THAT BRING YOU TO THE GALÁPAGOS

Chin, Jason. *Island: A Story of the Galápagos*. New York: Roaring Brook Press, 2012.

Hyde, Natalie. *Galápagos Islands Research Journal*. New York: Crabtree Publishing, 2018.

Messner, Kate. *Tracking Tortoises: The Mission to Save a Galápagos Giant*. Photographs by Jake Messner. Minneapolis: Millbrook, 2022.

Stine, Megan. *Where Are the Galápagos Islands?* New York: Grosset & Dunlap, 2017.

WEB RESOURCES TO INVESTIGATE

Darwin's Finches: https://galapagosconservation.org.uk/species/darwins-finches/

A website dedicated to the Galápagos Islands and their wildlife, including the many related species of finches

Evolution Explained: https://vimeo.com/96776961

A delightful CaravanLab video explanation of natural selection and evolution

Evolution in Action: Guppies: https://vimeo.com/96778347

Another delightful video exploration of evolution, this time through the natural selection of guppies in the wild

The Origin of Species: The Beak of the Finch: https://www.biointeractive.org/classroom-resources/origin-species-beak-finch

This Howard Hughes Medical Institute (HHMI) BioInteractive video brings viewers to the Galápagos and deep into the work of Peter and Rosemary Grant.

The Phylogenetic Tree of Anole Lizards: https://www.youtube.com/watch?v=rdZOwyDbyL0

This HHMI BioInteractive video further explores the process of evolution by natural selection, this time through the anole research of Dr. Jonathan Losos.

If you can locate a copy of the "What Darwin Never Saw" episode of the PBS show *The New Explorers*, hosted by Bill Kurtis, which aired on October 18, 1995, give it a watch! (Try the DVD section of your local library, or ask your librarian for help.)

Source Notes

p. 3: "[T]he water around Daphne . . . whales passing": B. Rosemary Grant, personal communication with the author, September 28, 2023.

p. 3: "I have had my toes . . . by an octopus": Grant, *Enchanted by Daphne*, 120.

p. 3: "Quite simply . . . magical": Achenbach.

p. 3: "It feels like . . . born there": ibid.

p. 21: "Selection doesn't . . . in your backyard": Weiner, 109.

Bibliography

Achenbach, Joel. "The People Who Saw Evolution." *Princeton Alumni Weekly*, April 23, 2014, accessed September 14, 2023. https://paw.princeton.edu/article/people-who-saw-evolution.

Beebe, William. *Galápagos: World's End*. Mineola, NY: Dover, 1988. First published 1924 by Putnam (New York).

Boag, Peter T. "Morphological Variation in the Darwin's Finches (*Geospizinae*) of Daphne Major Island, Galápagos." PhD thesis, Department of Biology, McGill University, May 1981.

Boag, Peter, and Peter R. Grant. "Intense Natural Selection in a Population of Darwin's Finches (*Geospizinae*) in the Galápagos." *Science* 214, no. 4516 (October 1981): 82–85.

Enroth, Christopher. "We've Been Genetically Altering Plants for Thousands of Years." *Good Growing* (blog), College of Agricultural, Consumer, and Environmental Sciences, University of Illinois, November 17, 2023. https://extension.illinois.edu/blogs/good-growing/2015-06-12-weve-been-geneetically-altering-plants-thousands-years.

Grant, Peter R. *Ecology and Evolution of Darwin's Finches*. Princeton: Princeton University Press, 1986.

———. *Enchanted by Daphne: The Life of an Evolutionary Naturalist*. Princeton: Princeton University Press, 2023.

Grant, Peter R., and K. Thalia Grant. "Breeding and Feeding Ecology of the Galápagos Dove." *Condor* 81, no. 4 (November 1979): 397–403. https://doi.org/10.2307/1366966.

Grant, Peter R., and Nicola Grant. "Breeding and Feeding of Galápagos Mockingbirds, *Nesomimus parvulus*." *Auk* 96, no. 4 (October 1979): 723–736. https://doi.org/10.1093/auk/96.4.723.

Grant, Peter R., and O. Rosemary Grant. *40 Years of Evolution: Darwin's Finches on Daphne Major Island*. Princeton: Princeton University Press, 2014.

Howard Hughes Medical Institute . "The Origin of Species: The Beak of the Finch." HHMI BioInteractive video, 15:54. https://www.biointeractive.org/classroom-resources/origin-species-beak-finch.

Losos, Jonathan. *Improbable Destinies: Fate, Chance, and the Future of Evolution*. New York: Riverhead, 2017.

Stewart, Paul D. *Galápagos: The Islands That Changed the World*. New Haven: Yale University Press, 2006.

Weiner, Jonathan. *The Beak of the Finch: A Story of Evolution in Our Time*. New York: Knopf, 1994.

Acknowledgments

The author would like to thank Dr. Jonathan Losos, professor, and Dr. Elizabeth Carlen, postdoctoral fellow, both at Washington University in St. Louis, for their thorough and patient review of the manuscript.

About the Author

Loree Griffin Burns is a biologist and the author of many nonfiction books for children, including the first book in the Discovery Chronicles, *One Long Line: Marching Caterpillars and the Scientists Who Followed Them.* Her books have won numerous accolades, including American Library Association Notable designations, a *Boston Globe–Horn Book* Honor, an IRA Children's Book Award, and a Green Earth Book Award, and have twice won the AAAS/Subaru Prize for Excellence in Science Books. She lives in New York, where she writes, teaches, and watches the birds in her backyard.

About the Illustrator

Jamie Green is the illustrator of multiple books for young readers, including the first book in the Discovery Chronicles, *One Long Line: Marching Caterpillars and the Scientists Who Followed Them*, and was the 2019 Society of Illustrators Zankel Scholar. Their work explores themes of science, history, fun, and all things that fly. Jamie Green lives just west of Chicago and can often be found foraging in local parks or lifting at the gym.